T0208395

YOUR GREAT NAME

SHAWN FUNK

authorHOUSE®

AuthorHouse™
1663 Liberty Drive
Bloomington, IN 47403
www.authorhouse.com
Phone: 833-262-8899

Published by AuthorHouse   05/04/2023

ISBN: 979-8-8230-0079-6 (sc)
ISBN: 979-8-8230-0080-2 (hc)
ISBN: 979-8-8230-0081-9 (e)

Library of Congress Control Number: 2023902196

Print information available on the last page.

This book is printed on acid-free paper.

Contents

Poem # *1*

The bards of old, their words relayed
And rocked their listeners from the stage
Those heartfelt lines by poet greats
Like Shakespeare, Chaucer, Blake and Yeats
Like how I've loved thee I'll count the ways
Those words like magic hold our gaze
Or seeing the world in a grain of sand
While holding eternity in our hand
A father's poem of years to come
Dancing to a frenzied drum
The knight's tale, a worthy man
And how his story first began
But none can best the man from Uz
Whose faith in God to Satan proved
No one can match this artist pen
When he describes Leviathan
"He makes the depths churn
Like a boiling cauldron
And stirs up the sea
Like a pot of ointment
Behind him he leaves a glistening wake
One would think
The deep had white hair"

Job 41:31

Poem # *2*

Just as a bride walks down the aisle
with gown and train and veiled smile
so, from above his bride descends
Where God himself will dwell with men
inside a glow of holy light
makes naught the need for moon filled nights
no fear of death or tearful cries
the lamb himself will wipe our eyes
Twelve gates of pearl surround all sides
in jeweled walls that reach the skies
inside are sights not dreamed by men
and God himself will dwell with them
a stream of life flows from the throne
its riverbanks are overgrown
with trees of life along both sides
that let men taste eternal lives

Poem # 3

Fearless men brought to their knees
By slashing rain and stormy seas
Calloused hands grip tight the oars
To fight the wind and waves that roar
Howling wind whips sea-soaked hair
Across their eyes filled with despair
Certain now they've breathed their last
As waters tower above the mast
With all hope gone they lift their gaze
And see the Godman walk the waves
He lifts his hand says, peace be still
As natures worse bows to his will
What man is this, their whispers say
That even the wind and waves obey
Four wonderous days he spent enthralled
Until he heard the master's call
Left behind were the tear-stained eyes
As sisters grieve and brother's cry
Friends and family gathered 'round
To mourn the man placed in the ground
At Jesus' feet the sisters cried
If you were here, he'd not have died
They took him where his friend was kept
Then deeply moved the Godman wept
His voice rang out so strong and clear
A sound that even the dead can hear
What man is this, their whispers say
That even the grave and death obey

Poem # 4

The heavens declare the glory of God
To us blessed men who walk this sod
The skies proclaim the works of his hands
As through the hourglass slips our sand
From before time the great "I AM"
Created the heavens as the angels sang
The vastness of space black as a slate
Gave room for the artist his works to create
Millions of stars in the canopy bright
Stage props in his play called northern lights
A river of green through the cold night skies
Its shoreline splashed with purple dyes
Explosions of colour erupt from the stream
Spectacular motion their unending theme
Wave upon wave in endless lines
Breathtaking in beauty and perfect design
He calls them forth to shimmer and dance
While holding us spellbound in a trance
He marshals their hosts assigning their place
The power of the maker in their beauty displayed

Poem # 5

Let there be light the word was spoken
Then bursting forth was stillness broken
Crashing waves and roaring seas
New mountain peaks take bended knees
His canyon carves and river wind
The ocean teems with brilliant kinds
The light of life his power displays
As earth takes shape like potter's clay
Let there be light and fiery stones
Blameless he dwelled around God's throne
Till pride and lies consumed his ways
He would not share his maker's praise
Darkness gloom and satan mocking
Foundation stone in pain is rocking
Night descends while heaven cries
Author of life and light has died
Let there be light the Son awakes
The stone is rolled its seal's break
Strides from the tomb as heaven sings
Death where's your victory, where's your sting
Darkness takes flight the day arrives
The light of life will flood the skies
Earth's curse removed it lends its voice
as cedars clap and rocks rejoice
Let there be light no need for sun
The prayer is heard thy kingdom come
The bride descends bedecked with stones
And in its midst is set God's throne
Rivers of life and streets of gold
An end of death and growing old
From mountain heights to ocean waves
The earth renewed will sings God's praise

Poem # 6

One day it came as sweet surprise
Like dawns first light flooding the skies
That spark of joy deep in my chest
I felt its heat and caught my breath
Like springtime's sun ends winter freeze
So, my heart melted from the breeze
That drifted through my frozen life
As God's love melts away my strife
As water diamonds catch the light
When fish break free and near take flight
So, my heart and soul will rise
When God relents and hears my cries
We ask in faith for healing wings
Which God in mercy swiftly brings
He listens to the heart that is broke
Then softly says let's share the yoke

Poem # 7

In the garden God searched for man
As he walked in the cool of day the day
And then as now they hid and ran
And hoped he'd look the other way
They hid amidst the leaves and boughs
As God called out, Where art thou
To spread his word God found a man
To warn them of a coming day
And then as now he hid and ran
And hoped he'd look the other way
In towering waves about to drown
To God he called, where art thou
To earth God came a humble man
To usher in a brand-new day
And then as now the demons ran
And hoped he look the other way
As darkness settled like a shroud
To God he called, where art thou
Behind cold stone, they laid the man
As all creations counts the days
God sent his word and angles ran
And worshipped when he looked their way
Now death's sting before him bows
As God calls out, where art thou

Poem # 8

What sights and sounds my spirits lift
And bring to mind my saviours gifts
The softness of my lover's skin
Her kisses sweet as cinnamon
The scent of pine upon the wind
Driving rain on roofs of tin
Sails taunt against the breeze
Blossom laden apple trees
The whistle as a killdeer sings
The flutter of a monarch's wings
Blazing speed on fresh cut grass
A winning goal or perfect pass
The laughter in my young sons' eyes
Winged V's in flight through autumn skies
My daughter's hugs when off to bed
Their gentle love you's softly said
Floodgates open blessings pour
On undeserved who love the Lord

Poem # 9

I often think my Lord displayed
A crooked smile or laughing eyes
When dealing with his jars of clay
I think he loved to get a rise
Like when his friends clung to a boat
Certain they were going to die
Praying it would stay afloat
It says he just came walking by
Or when a man filled with hot air
Said in your eye a speck I see
The Lord said you ought not to stare
While in your eye there is a beam
The time the girls were filled with grief
He must have thought what should be said
To make their face flood with relief
He said the living aren't with the dead
Froze with fear the doors locked tight
The Lord appeared inside the room
Now what to say to ease their fright
I sure could use some honeycomb
He came to earth to do God will
And met with men in massive crowds
While all the prophets he fulfilled
Sometimes I think he laughed out loud

Poem # *10*

I search to find the perfect words
And set them in a poet's frame
Their power leaping off the page
In verse that glorifies his name
The reader's heart is swept away
To learn the truth of why he came
He left his throne and father's side
All for the glory of his name
The heavens filled with angels
As shepherds heard them praise
They searched the barns of Bethlehem
And glorified his name
He lived and loved among us
Cured the sick and healed the lame
Raised the dead and saved the dying
All for the glory of his name
He bravely faced the cross before him
His final breath was filled with pain
For love he paid the price to save us
All for the glory of his name
Three long nights it tried to hold him
As life did battle with the grave
Death couldn't keep its grip upon him
The empty tomb now sings his praise

Poem # *11*

With frenzied cries they call to Baal
As by their god they were betrayed
Then from his knees Elijah prayed
And Gods reply from heaven fell
From deep within that kingly lair
His life upon the balance hangs
To save his life from the lion's fangs
In faith believed God answers prayer
Beaten, bound and thrown in jail
Paul and Silas sang and prayed
Guards and jailors stand amazed
As heavens court arranges bail
Men of renown in days gone by
Gave witness so that we might see
Our prayers are heard from bended knees
When with our hearts to you we cry

Poem # *12*

The skies dissolve and heavens rent
As one last time the Son is sent
In awe stands satans mighty horde
At stallions, trumps and flashing swords
No donkey's foal or bed of straw
His back laid bare the flesh cut raw
No swaddling clothes or crown of thorns
This time he's come as Lord of Lords
Fear and rage their bodies numb
Too late they shout, God's wrath has come
Kings and slaves alike will cry
To mountain crags please let us die
As lightning flashes from the east
The king arrives to slay the beast
Take back his earth and start his reign
And rid the world of death and pain
The earth will fill with his renown
As elders bow and their crowns
With shouts of joy from seraphim
The cherubs sing their praise to him

Poem # 13

I got my first true glimpse of grace
I couldn't look straight in his face
Even the stones a shroud required
But with the new they were retired
We hold our sin in such esteem
Like it could ever come between
That flickering wick, that tolling bell
Is quenched beneath his oceans swell
Those waves of grace that tower high
Sweep up my prayers as they roll by

Poem # *14*

With his word, the heavens rent
And spread the cosmos like a tent
He spoke the double helix strand
And breathed the very breath of man
With tilts and planes, he made the seasons
By grace endowed the mind with reason
I've heard him called both lamb and lion
And also called the king of Zion
When someone asked him for his name
He simply said I am "I Am"

Poem # *15*

Empty tomb with deaths sting stolen
That sealed stone was rock and roll'n
Eyes ablaze'n third day raise'n our
Soul save'n one and only Son of God
Filled with power and with grace
He came to save the human race
That father talk'n water walk'n demon
Toss'n one and only son of God
Now all the elders cast their crowns
As heaven rumbles with the sound
The trumpet ring'n angels sing'n
Holy, holy one and only Son of God
He's coming back with a two edged sword
As kings of kings and Lord of Lords
That angel guide'n stallion ride'n
Death and defy'n one and only son of God
The root of David Juda's Lion
Returns in triumph to mount Zion
Mountains shake'n satan quake'n
Dread of face'n the one and only Son of God

Poem # *16*

If I could sweep wide histories curtain
Peering down through time I'm certain
Unveiling epic loves of yore
Your love would rival them and more
In verse we read of mounds of Myrrh
Seductive words that speak of her
The wise kings love for Sheba's Queen
Revealed in words we read between
Bacall and Bogey made us dream
While Liz and Rich lit movie screens
Robinhood with merry men
He risked it all for Miriam
Cleopatra took the sting
The next in line gave up the king
All for the love the legends grow
Per chance too bold, I say I know
I know the love that can't be earned
Though how or why I've yet to learn
God sent my love, my beauty Queen
I'm blessed to love you my Raileen

Poem # 17

A mother's words worth more than gold
As gems within her words unfold
Like buried treasure brought to light
With her choice words we find delight
Like porch lights as the evening fell
Or shimmering coins within a well
Like honey dripping from its comb
Or knowing that your almost home
Her wisdom lends its healing balm
In soothing words that bring such calm
More priceless than a laden chest
Her words like silk they give us rest
A precious gift her children hold
A mother's words worth more than gold

Poem # *18*

Made in his image his father's son
Striking resemblance, the two could be one
Stare at his picture as thought drift away
Would I be as brave if I faced that day
Memories stir some proud and some sad
Could I play the hero just like my dad
Five little children and a beautiful wife
For love of another he laid down his life
A short swim to shore not too far away
His love for his brother forced him to stay
A verse has been penned I quite admire
It's found in the book my God has inspired
"No greater love hath this, that a man lay
down his life to save another"

John 15:13

Poem # *19*

There is a bond that binds two hearts
That's never meant to break apart
A silver cord that both loves feel
Like spiders' silk of liquid steel
But there's a shock that steals your breath
When loves betrayed its worse than death
When your heart pleads to make her say
That she won't take her love away
We know that times supposed to heal
That place inside that used to feel
But now that's just an empty space
That frozen time cannot erase
It hits hard and knocks you down
Until your knees are on the ground
But that's not where you're going to stay
Something inside wont work that way

Poem # *20*

The greatest of gifts
From God I possess
The love of my children
With which I am blessed
One lights up a room
With the glow of her smile
Ones heart is so gentle
Caring and mild
My youngest just five
Its already quite clear
The sort of young man
That soon will appear
He's brave as a lion
And ready to fight
Eyes full of laughter
Shining and bright
The love of my children
A gift from above
To me they are proof
That my God is love

Poem # *21*

I watch your lips curl
From a smile to a pout
Your tiny brow wrinkles
Your fist flail about
Awake for an instant
With a flash of blue eyes
That drift back to dream
With your soft baby sighs
For your tiny perfection
I wasn't prepared
To me you are proof
That God answers prayers

Poem # *22*

Beautiful angel from the outside in
To steal a line from a music king
Still others write of doe's and doves
To tell the world about their love
The readers hearts are gently stirred
When they see those picture words
My daughter's love is more compared
To priceless stones and gems, so rare
Her beauty fills her dad with pride
And prouder still for what's inside
When all my world was cold and dark
The ones I loved had closed their hearts
Then her love like a beacon flared
And calmed a storm, I couldn't bare
With iron will, she sets her bounds
With inner strength she stands her ground
Of self-doubt, there's not a trace
As she blends perfect love and grace
From the first day we got our start
Your saucer blue eyes just stole my heart
I'm filled with pride for all you've done
And for the lady you've become

Poem # *23*

Poetic lines and sweet refrains
Convey the love my heart contains
But they will never do justice
To make you feel my love for you
A timeless bond I didn't know
Between a dad and son could grow
My priceless gift from God above
That lets me feel a father's love
If ever I was forced to choose
My life to keep or you to lose
Without your love or without breath
A broken heart would be my death
A wasted life but for the sight
Of laughing eyes that glisten bright
Across the room we share a glance
Inside my chest I feel it dance
There are no words that I can speak
Just saying love would sound too weak
Your soul and mine complete a ring
And makes mine soar on eagle's wings

Poem # 24

That beauty kicked back on the deck
Both hands filled with smooth Malbec
Her smile makes my poor head spin
But reds not all that I drank in
Because I found my love again
Reds not all I'm drinking in
Her name was Rai just like the sun
With just one look I came undone
That red sundress was cotton thin
But reds not all I'm drinking in
The deck was rocking with the waves
And keeping time, her body swayed
The red sun sets as night begins
But reds not all I'm drinking in
She laughed like silk and shook her head
As Chris De Burgh sang lady red
We raised our glass to toast again
But reds not all I'm drinking in
Because I found my love again
Reds not all I'm drinking in

Poem # 25

Sometimes I feel all undone
And the words won't seem to come
Sometimes they flow as smooth as wine
And fill the pages of my mind
My goal to thread that perfect line
With latticed words of love entwined
Word like beauty, grace and blessed
Wine and fire and hearts undressed
A line that weaves and binds our souls
And makes two halves become one whole
That's how it feels to breathe you in
When were so close we share one skin

Poem # *26*

I'd love more than X & O's
But that's as far as you can go
You had your heart broke once before
You're making sure it wont no more
Still, I'll take what you can give
Those X & O's are why I live
I'll love you till the end of days
And hope someday to hear you say
You know our love took its own path
But that's what's going to make it last
Until that time, I hope you know
I love to hear those X & O's
When at last your heart is free
Then you can let yourself believe
My loves not here to hurt and steal
And you believe my loves for real
I hope God gives us countless days
For all the love you's left to say
For far too long I didn't know
How priceless were your X & O's

Poem # 27

The barn still stands how we left it that day
Old rafters and memories, lofts of stale hay
I walk through the doors like stepping through time
Yesteryears ghosts brush down my spine
Forty-six years since I stood in that mow
The silence feels sacred like keeping a vow
We all stand together yet each stand alone
And smile at the memories that made this our home
Of brothers and preachers and backflips in hay
And staticky songs that our radio played
The branch that God raised by his own design
He knew that his strength came from the vine
The paths that we followed that led us back here
That day in the barn were so crystal clear

Poem # *28*

Faith, it's said can mountains move
A short list follows here to prove
All these men of faith and fame
Through the ages left their name
By faith, Abel brought his best
By faith, Daniel past the test
Fire and Lions caused no fear
God's own angel hovered near
By faith, Enoch wasn't found
By faith, Jericho fell down
Around the walls for seven days
Gods command they did obey
By faith, Rahab hid the spies
By faith, Abraham bound and tied
His true love, his only son
Promised heir the chosen one
By faith, Noah built his boat
By faith, was Moses set afloat
Fearing God, they did decide
Pharaoh's orders to defy
Of their faith, there is no doubt
But there's one name that's been left out
All the faith that these men knew
Is echoed by my mother to
Lost her man and first born son
Enough to shatter anyone
Blinding pain and pure heartache
She would not her God forsake
Faith that makes a mountain move
Faith that all your pain will soothe
Faith that made the red sea part
Rests within my mother's heart

Poem # *29*

Have you heard about the story
The one about five thousand fed
It tells of our savior's power
Told in letters, wrote in red
My soul neither will go hungry
My lord is my daily bread
Just spend some time inside the book
And read the letters wrote in red
In days of old, Rahab was told
To hang that Scarlett coloured thread
That crimson cord God's mercy showed
And matched the letters wrote in red
Jonah to was told to go
It filled him with the deepest dread
Hard lesson learned, obey your God
Now told in letters, wrote in red
So, when looking for some answers
Wondering what the master said
Take some time to crack the book
And read the letters wrote in red
He will always guide and lead you
If you place your lord ahead
Just cast all your cares upon him
And read the letters wrote in red

Poem # *30*

In the beginning was the word
Long before the earth and sky
He took on flesh and dwelled among us
As angels sang his praise on high
When I feel space between us
My restless heart just wants you more
The only place I go to find you
Is in the pages of your word
When my soul is dry and thirsty
Your face is all I long to see
Like water gushing from the rock
Your words come rushing over me
The hours pass inside the pages
My spirit soothes to see your might
Then I take your yoke upon me
Cling to your words my burdens light
When I feel my grasp is slipping
My wayward heart drifts far away
Then I recall, its you that holds me
And that your word won't let me stray
They say the balms in Gilead
His comfort spreads across the ages
They say he rides on healing wings
Still, I trust only in the pages

Poem # *31*

Lord let me see the hills abound
With your angels that surround
Unveil my eyes to angel throngs
Standing guard in faith that's strong
Lift my eyes to see their camp
And hear them praise God's only lamb
Open my eyes to let me see
How far your love extends to me
When life's worries overflow
Let me then be still and know
Open my eyes to let me see
Great is the love that covers me

Poem # *32*

The youngest son so far from home
His friends surround, yet he's alone
His thoughts drift back before he strayed
With all hope gone he wished he'd stayed
Fallen too far outside God's plan?
While still far off the father ran
The father watched day after day
And hoped his son would kneel and pray
From far off lands, he finally came
To bare his soul and rid his shame
Would God yet hear this broken man?
While still far off the father ran
Waves of love with joy he cried
My son was dead now, he's alive
All heavens host sing sweet refrain
The wayward son is home again
Did God forgive this fallen man?
While still far off the father ran

Poem # *33*

Before my God, satan stands
His poisoned voice accusing
This man proclaimed
Your holy name
Then lost his way like shifting sand
But then God spoke, "my work is done"
As heavens thunder rolled
Lay not your hand
Upon this man
"Now give me back my son"
I've got him now he's lost to you
His voice was robbed in evil
His sins too great
He's sealed his fate
There's nothing more that you can do
But then God spoke "my work is done"
As all of heavens kneels in awe
With eyes that blazed
He held his gaze
"Now give me back my son"
You can't forgive it isn't right
The liar's voice was raging
His love for you
Was never true
Ban him forever from your sight
But then God spoke "My work is done"
As angels sang his praises
Now for all time, all power is mine
"Now give me back my son"

Poem # *34*

What depths of love
It must have been
That made the word take flesh
And let his blood
Flow down the tree
So, I need not taste death
And never could
This sinful man
Draw nearer to your throne
Without that crimson covering
You shed for me alone
Behold the spotless
Lamb of God
Whose death tore down the wall
Now covered by your precious blood
I feel your mercies fall

Poem # *35*

Peter swore he didn't know
And that the man he'd never met
But when he heard the rooster crow
Their eyes were locked, and peter wept
His tortured soul felt so heartsick
But once again God's mercy showed
Now what to do with Hebrews six
When God decides his love will flow
The youngest son left home for years
Living life for friends and fame
His loving dad he brought to tears
With no one but himself to blame
Through pigs and mud, husks and sticks
God again his mercy showed
Now what to do with Hebrews six
When God decides his love will flow
Another's wife he stole away
The carefully laid his evil plan
Her husband he would cruelly slay
So, he could be Bathsheba's man
Through Nathan, God his conscience pricked
And once again God's mercy showed
Now what to do with Hebrews six
When God decides his love will flow
These two men and the youngest son
All loved their God, then fell away
With broken hearts for what they'd done
They turned to God and knelt to pray
I know no sin that God can't fix
And once again Gods mercy shows
Now what to do with Hebrews six
When God decides his love will flow

Poem # *36*

I learned the verse while still a boy
He came to seek and save the lost
It filled me with such peace and joy
My debt he paid at such a cost
But how does death affect a child
When dad and brother find the grave
Who knew the pain behind the smile
That led me to a life depraved
Until beyond mercy's domain
For certain I was falling
Then for the glory of your name
I gently heard you calling
With head bowed low and eyes that wept
My broken heart implored these
Was then I learned of mercies depth
As love in waves restored me

Poem # *37*

The psalmist says he wont reject
A contrite and a broken heart
God only knows the pain in mine
As past mistakes tear it apart
If he says I fell too far
When I see him face to face
Then I'll agree that he is just
When he assigns me to my place
But if it really is for all sin
That the spotless lamb was slain
Then I know that when I see him
He will put to rest my shame
So unworthy of his presence
Still in my heart is one wish only
To hear the angels 'round his throne
Singing holy, holy, holy
Until that day at last arrives
Within my heart I hold his word
His mercy like a river flows
The sweetest sound I ever heard

Poem # *38*

From heavens throne he saw the need
He was appalled that there was none
No one on earth to intercede
And so, he sent his only Son
Revealed in awesome splendid power
As stars and angels sang for joy
At last, has come his kingdoms hour
Within the person of a boy
He is the author of the verse
That fills me with a quiet peace
It eases pain from sins cruel curse
Delivers joy and sweet release
It is about a man forgiven
Whose sin the lord has swept away
A verse about a man who's risen
To rid a debt, I could not pay
"I have swept your offenses away like a cloud.
Your sins like the morning mist" Isa 44:21

Poem # *39*

High above the valley floor
Stands the mountain of the lord
That special place that sacred stone
Where God will one day raise his throne
The heart of God is always there
To hear my broken-hearted prayer
On that stone the son was tied
While in his heart the father cried
Still in faith he raised his sword
That righteous man who loved the lord
Until Gods heart that's always there
Heard his broken-hearted prayer
To that place I made my way
Believing God would hear me pray
On trembling knees, I called his name
In search of him who rids my shame
And to my joy, Gods heart was there
To hear my broken-hearted prayer
Always before me, day and night
But now they're hidden from his sight
As mornings mist gives way at dawn
From God's eyes my sins are gone
Because God's heart was always there
To hear my broken-hearted prayer

Printed in the United States
by Baker & Taylor Publisher Services